A
DO
SOMETHING
MAN

CHOOSING GREAT IN YOUR LIFE

A DO SOMETHING MAN

CHOOSING GREAT IN YOUR LIFE

ROGERS W. JACKSON
B.A., M.DIV., TH.M., D.MIN.

CRONOS PRESS

A
DO
SOMETHING
MAN
CHOOSING GREAT IN YOUR LIFE

Copyright © 2012

ROGERS W. JACKSON,
Rogers Jackson Ministries, Inc.

Website: www.RogersJackson.com
Email: rogersjackson@comcast.net
(773) 490 -7269

ISBN: 978-1-60414-543-4

Cronos Press is in imprint of Fideli Publishing Inc.

www.FideliPublishing.com

Dedication

To Coach Lester Beene
Ft. Worth Dunbar, Football Head Coach, 1974

"Coach, I want to play Middle Linebacker!"

"Jackson, you are to slow to play Middle
Linebacker.

"Do you know why you want to be Middle
Linebacker?"

"Why Coach?"

"You're selfish! You don't want to help the team,
you want glory for yourself.

"If you play where I put you, the ball will come to
you! You can both help the team win and get
all the glory you desire!"

Dr. Robert Moore
"Make a boy your Project."
Professor, Chicago Theological Seminary, Chicago

Lacey Kirk Curry, IL
Edward O. Williamson, NY
Sonny Adolph, MS, Mark Williamson, MS
Larry Tyler, IL, Nathaniel Allison, IL
George Waddles, Sr., IL, Scott Onque
Richard House, IL, Cleveland Thomas, IL
Nathaniel Randle, IL, Walter Turner III, IL
Henry Barlow, IL
Michael A. Bell, TX, Bruce Datcher, TX
Larry Sanders, TX, Chester Williams, TX
Reginald Reynolds, TX, Robert L. Rogers, TX
Richard J. Rose, TX
Avan Odom, OH

*"Every Man cannot do everything,
but every Man can do something.
The something, and the one thing that
that Man can do,
He must do to glorify God
and benefit others."*

— ROGERS W. JACKSON

Contents

1. CHOOSING GREAT IN YOUR LIFE 3

    Choose the Highway 4

    Great by Choice 5

    Helping Others into Great 7

    Choosing the Low Road 8

    Choose Great 10

    The Right Choice 12

2. AN APPROVED MAN 15

    Reproved, Improved, and Approved 15

    Biblical Approval 16

    Study to Be Approved 18

    Approved Unto God 19

3. A NO EXCUSE MAN 23

    Realizations 24

    Making Excuses 25

    Excuse defined 27

    Man Made Excuses 27

    A No Excuse Man has Peace 31

4. A DO SOMETHING MAN 35

Making the Play.. 36
Be Instructed to Do Something 37
The Why of Instruction 38
The Bible's Do Something 39
Do the Necessary 42
Men who Did Something 43

5. A SUCCESSFUL MAN 47

Biblical Success... 48
Getting Out of Average..................................... 50
Moving Toward Success 50
State Your Goal 51
Push Beyond Average 54

ENDNOTES... 57

BIBLIOGRAPHY 63

CHAPTER 1

Choosing Great in Your Life

*"We cannot predict the future.
But we can create it."[1]*

*"God has gifted men in each generation,
to take action, and do something great.
Now is not the time to be submissive."*

— MICHAEL FLETCHER

On Sunday, December 25, 2011, Christmas Day, the Chicago Bulls played the Los Angeles Lakers in the Staples Center. Coach Tom Thibodaux stated that Derrick Rose is a game winner. To move from good to great, Thibodeau suggests that *"you must have the courage to take the next shot."*[2]

To Move from Good to Great, become an "**Encore Man**." An "Encore Man" does **again and again** what needs to be done. To "choose great" in your life, consider the following:

1. Develop a great resolve to find a way to win.
2. Lead by actions.
3. Come early, stay late, practice hard.
4. Give it everything you have and never quit.
5. Be the primary option.[3]

"Great players, you're not going to stop them."[4]

A. Choose the Highway

In the poem, "The Ways," John Oxenham calls us to "**Choose**" the highway. Listen to his words:

> To every Man there openeth, a [high way and a low]... And the **high soul** takes the **high [way]** and the **low soul** take the **low**, and **in between** on the **misty flats**, the **rest drift to and fro**; But to **every[man]** there **openeth** a **highway** and a **low**, and **every[man must choose** which]... way his soul shall go.[5]

To "**Be Great**," you must **Not** "**Settle**," and "**Be Satisfied**" in your present state of being and condition. Choose not to wait for tomorrow to shape you. Shape your tomorrow by choosing the "Great Things" of God.

The great (gadol) things of God are those significant actions of God that bring redemption[6] and restoration.

Choose the redemptive purposes of God for your life that will benefit the world.

B. Great by Choice

"Set the Tone."

—TOM THIBODEAU,
HEAD COACH, CHICAGO BULLS

"Being Little" is a "Choice" just as "Being Great" is a "Choice." Being *"little"* is to be *filled* with *"self-getting"* and *"self-serving."* To be *"great"* is to *"serve others".* The Lord Jesus declared, in **Mark 10:43**: *"But ... whosoever will be great among you, shall be your minister."* When you Choose Great, you have chosen to be on a Ministry Team that helps others Win.

"Focus on the job at hand,
always placing the team above self."[7]

— GEORGE MCCASKEY
CHICAGO BEARS CHAIRMAN

To push Men out of Good into Great, be a minister that focuses on the job of putting others before yourself. What does the Lord Jesus mean when He said, "whosoever will be great among you shall be your minister?"

1. To *minister (sarat)* is to *serve*.
2. To *minister (sarat)* means to be *the chief assistant*.
3. To *minister (sarat)* is to *fulfill* the *role of a priest*.[8]
4. To *minister (diakoneo)* is to *give help* and *bring* the *advantage* to others.[9]

You are called by the Lord Jesus Christ to **serve**, **assist**, to **be priestly**, and to **give others the advantage**. Focus on putting others ahead of you to help the team win.

THINK ABOUT IT!

Tell how you assisted someone today _____

_____.

C. Helping Others into Great

"Make sure that everyone is moving forward."[10]

— GEORGE MCCASKEY

In an article, Phil Emery the general manager for the Chicago Bears said,

> I'm here to help this team. I'm a teammate. Yes, I'm in a leadership role, but I'm here to provide support, help, guidance and talent toward winning ..."[11]

No Man is able to move from Good to Great without "help." Each Man is called to be the "***help'*** that another Man needs to move toward God's potential for his life. Every godly Man is "Called to Be the Leader."

1. Lead by "***providing support***." Name your support role _____.

2. Lead by "***giving help***." Name the help you gave someone today _____.

3. Lead by "***offering guidance***." Who needs your guidance today? _____

4. Lead by "***enabling Men to win***." What Man needs a win in his life? _____

"When you are focused on goals ... and ... want to be part of a team ... and part of something positive ... sometimes the impossible is achieved."[12]

— PHIL EMERY,
CHICAGO BEARS GENERAL MANAGER

THINK ABOUT IT!

Share one goal you can set to move a Man to achieve

Great _____.

D. Choosing the Low Road

*"... the high soul takes the high [way]
and the low soul take the low ..."*

— JOHN OXENHAM

1. Sam Hurd

In the Saturday, December 17, 2011 issue of the *Chicago Sun Times,* is the story of a *"**self-serving man**."* The headline read, *"Busted Bear Released from Jail - And from Team."* **Sam Hurd** played five seasons with the **Dallas Cowboys**. The Chicago Bears made a three year, **$5.1 million dollar** deal with Hurd.[13]

Instead of choosing Great, Sam Hurd choose "Less than Great." Now the name of **Sam Hurd** is connected with **shame**.

> Sam Hurd, 26, faces charges that he intended to conspire to distribute 500 grams of cocaine which carries a penalty of 40 years in prison and up to a $5 million dollar fine. As a result of the charges against him, the Chicago Bears cut him from the team.[14]

As a Christian, you are called to choose "Great." You must meet the chaos, the uncertainty, and the challenges of your moments by "doing something."

Envy thou not the oppressor, and choose none of his ways."

— PROVERBS 3:31

2. Rod Blagojevich

Former convicted Illinois Governor, Rod Blagojevich had the desire to be great. He choose "a way," and thus his life drifted "to and fro on the misty flats of life." He did not choose to "undertake the works of God" that would magnify and grow others.

Rod Blagojevich choose "*political corruption*" and was given the "stiffest sentence imposed for political corruption in Illinois history."[15] On **18 counts for corruption** along with trying to sell the vacated U.S. Senate seat of Barack Obama, the judge said, "You did that damage."[16] After the verdict, **Mr. Blagojevich** said,

> I have nobody to blame but myself for my stupidity and actions... . They convicted me because those were my actions... . I was the governor; and I should have known better.[17]

The word of God can help us to "know better" and do better.

E. Choose Great

*"He never has been and never will be
a great one-on-one defender.
There is often hesitation on his part ..."*[18]

— NEIL HAYES, SPORTS WRITER
REFLECTING ON CARLOS BOOZER, CHICAGO BULLS PLAYER

What is the commentary that others have given, and are giving about your contribution to the game of life? Has anyone said "to your face," or "behind your back," — "He never has been and never will be great ... There is often hesitation on his part ..."

You can choose to *hesitate*, or you can choose to *participate* in the work that God has for your life. **Great is a Choice**. Choosing "**Average**" is not the intention of God for your life. In the book, *Great by Choice,* Collins and Hansen affirm that *you must choose* to *"perform exceptionally well"* or *"underperform."*[19]

Often our lives choose "less" than the Lord's best for us. In *Genesis 12:2*, the Lord said to *Abram*, at 75 years old, "And I will make of thee *a great nation*, and *I will bless thee*, and *make thy name great*; and *thou shalt be a blessing*." The Lord wants to work in your life and push you into Great.

To live your life in Great, consider the following actions you must live by daily:

1. *"Create"* instead of *"reacting."*
2. *"Prevail"* instead of trying to *"survive."*
3. *"Succeed,"* and *"Thrive"* in the purposes of God.
4. In the face of *"storms*, ... *shocks*, and ... *uncertainty* ... *endure."*[20]

God has put into your heart a **Do Something Great** mindset. Do Something!

THINK ABOUT IT!

What is the great God has put into your life today?

_____

> *"And Joshua answered them,*
> *If thou be a great people,*
> *then get thee up to the wood country ..."*
>
> **— JOSHUA 17:15**

To choose Great, "Get Up!" and "Do Something" that is **God desired** and **God preferred**.

1. To *choose (bahar) great* is to *select* what is *desirable*[21] *to God.*

2. To *choose (haireo) great* is to *take* for oneself *what is preferred*[22] by the Lord.

3. To *choose great (gadal)* is to *undertake the works of God* that makes something *important*[23] for *God's glory* and the benefit of others.

THINK ABOUT IT!

Name one work of God you will choose today to glorify God _____.

F. The Right Choice

To choose (qabal) great is to undertake willingly *the task*[24] *of the Lord.*

The Right Choice is to "choose" what the gracious Lord has chosen for you. Joshua, in the closing days of his leadership, called the people of Israel to choose the Lord. **Joshua 24:15** says, "*... choose you this day whom ye will serve. ... but as for me and my house, we will serve the LORD*" (Joshua 24:15).

THINK ABOUT IT!

Write one reason you will choose God's great _____

_____.

CHAPTER 2

An Approved Man

*An Approved Man "display[s] the fierce resolve
to do whatever [is] needed
to be done to make [others] great.*[25]

To *choose (haireo) great* in your life is to take for yourself **what is preferred**[26] **by God**. The good news is that the Lord Jesus prefers you. To be a *preferred (ginomai)* Man is to be **ready to be advanced** to any *station or office* to which you are appointed[27] by God. In order to advance from Good to Great, you must be discipled to be able to stand where the Lord places you.

A. Reproved, Improved, and Approved

You must be a discipled Man to move into Great. Discipleship is the *process* of *being Reproved, Improved, and Approved* for *God's initiative* in your life.

1. A discipled Man is a **Reproved** *(tokehah)* Man. A **Reproved** *(tokehah)* Man is one who is open to correction[28] and betterment.

2. A **Reproved** Man is an **Improved** Man. An **Improved** Man is *made better* for the work of God.

3. An **Improved Man** becomes a **Man Approved by God** who is continually being *trained to be qualified* for the *place* he is to complete the work of the Lord.

An **Approved Man** is *disciple (matheteuo)* who is *instructed*[29] in the mission of God. An **Approved Man** will *"deny himself,"* by saying *"No"* to *"his agenda,"* and will say *"Yes"* to *"Lord's agenda"* for his life.

THINK ABOUT IT!

Give one reason you must be discipled from Good to Great _____.

B. Biblical Approval

> *"Salute **Apelles approved** in Christ."*
>
> ROMANS 16:10

Appelles is a Man who joined the apostle Paul in the work of the Lord. *Apelles'* name means *"excluded and separated,"*[30] yet he is *included* and *approved*, in the biblical record, for the work and ministry of the Lord. How many Men do you know who are excluded from the mission of God for their lives? Write the name of an *"excluded and separated"* Man _____.
Your Mission is to help that Man to be *"Approved by God"* to *Achieve the Greatness* that God has for his life.

Reflect on the following scriptures concerning an Approved Man.

ACTS 2:22

*"... hear these words; Jesus of Nazareth, **a man approved of God** among you by **miracles** and **wonders** and **signs**, which God did by him."*

ROMANS 14:18

*"For he that ... **serveth** Christ is **acceptable to God**, and **approved** of men."*

1 CORINTHIANS 16:3

*"And when I come, whomsoever ye shall **approve** ... them will I send ..."*

THINK ABOUT IT!

Discuss why a *disapproved Man* is not sent on God's

mission _____.

C. Study to Be Approved

"Achieve greatness or perish."[31]

In **2 Timothy 2:15**, the apostle Paul says, *"Study to shew thyself **approved** unto God, a **workman** that needeth not to be ashamed ..."* To be an **Approved Man**, you must **study** and **move beyond good enough.** The Lord desires "More" from you, and calls you to be "**His disciple**" to move you from Good to Great.

An **Approved Man** will Study the Word of the Lord.

1. To *study (lahag)* is to *give devotion to examining*[32] the *work* that must be *done*. Challenge Men to study what God's assignment is for their life _____.

2. To *study (hagah)* is to *meditate on God's word* day and night[33] to know the work you are to do.

   Studying God's word gives us God's purpose for our work _____.

3. To *study (philotimeomai)* is to have *a love ambition* to make *the word of God* your *friend.*[34]

   Share one reason some Men have *a little love ambition* for the Lord's word _____.

THINK ABOUT IT!

Name the work that you must study for that must

be done _____.

D. Approved Unto God

"... shew thyself approved unto God..."

— 2 TIMOTHY 2:15

What does it mean to be *"approved unto God?"* To
be **approved (apodeiknumi) unto God** means to be one
who **demonstrates** and **exhibits** the **skills needed** to be
appointed to any office or **station**.[35] Write a skill that
you need to be appointed to a "service" station _____

_____.

"... approve things that are excellent."

— PHILIPPIANS 1:10

THINK ABOUT IT!

Write one thing in your life that demonstrated your

approval for service _____.

1. Confirmed by God

To be *approved (apodeiknumi) unto God* means to be *confirmed by God* with *power* to *accomplish* the *things God's chooses*.[36] Your approval by God is not for you to do what you desire to do. You are *Approved by God*, and given God's power, to do what God wants done.

To be **Approved by God**, today and tomorrow, you must be taught and trained, night and day, in God's word for your life mission.

The **Approval of God**, in your work, will be seen in *the power the Lord gives you* to accomplish what you have been assigned to do to glorify the Lord and benefit others.

THINK ABOUT IT!

Write one thing the Lord has approved you for in the mission of the Church_____.

2. Tested by Trial

To be *approved (dokimazo)* is to be *tested* and *examined* by *trial* and *difficulty*.[37] Name the trial and the difficulty that is shaping you for the work of the Lord _____.

To be *approved (dokimazo)* is to be **tested** by any other method **to bring the good in you out** that you might **be useful**.[38] *Daniel* was **approved by God** in the lion's den. A *disciple*, to be **approved** by God, is under *continuous examination* by *fire and trial* to be beneficial to others and the purposes of God.

THINK ABOUT IT!

Name the "good" the Lord is bringing out of your

life _____.

3. Tested in the Furnace of Adversity

To be *approved (dokimos)* is to **be tested** as metals, in the *fiery furnace of adversity*.[39] You cannot live in life without adversity and difficulty. Use the difficulty as a learning tool to strengthen you for the greater work the Lord has for you.

Look at the *furnace of adversity* that the three Hebrew Men faced. In **Daniel 3:17–26**, Shadrach, Meshach, and Abednego were approved by God in the fiery furnace. They were approved of being Men of Faith that had the testimony, "God is Able."

21

THINK ABOUT IT!

Name a testimony you have gained since coming through yesterday's fire of adversity _____.

An **Approved Man** is one who is *taught and instructed* in the *furnace of adversity to benefit others*. Without *study*, *instruction*, and *adversity*, a Man cannot move from Good to Great in any office or station where he is placed.

THINK ABOUT IT!

Tell why every Man must be approved for their qualified task _____.

> *"Some Men do not want to be taken into great.*
> *They are satisfied with their here,*
> *and are unwilling to move*
> *to God's here, there and yonder."*
>
> **— ROGERS JACKSON**

CHAPTER 3

A No Excuse Man

"It was a very hard-fought game.
We fought to the end. We just came up a little bit short.
We kind of ran out of time."[40]

— TOM BRADY, QUARTERBACK
NEW ENGLAND PATRIOTS, SUPER BOWL 46

" ... they are without excuse."

— ROMANS 1:20D

Often my life is filled with Excuses. We are often satisfied with "good enough." To do better, we must ask, "How can I do better tomorrow?" To "*do better*," Jim Collins and Jerry Porras, in their chapter, "*Good Enough Never Is*," state that we must **develop a habit of mind** and **action** that is **never ending** to improve your future.[41]

A. Realizations

1. Realize that you never have it made.[42]

2. Realize that "contentment will lead to complacency, which inevitably leads to decline."[43]

3. Realize that you must keep alive the fire that pushes people to never be satisfied.[44]

4. Realize that you "cannot run, hide, evade, or procrastinate"[45] your responsibility.

5. "Beat yesterday ... never stop trying to improve."[46]

In their 2011 run for the National Basketball Championship, the Chicago Bulls were eliminated by the Miami Heat. Carlos Boozer, of the Bulls, in an article titled, "Boozer Driven by Criticism," has stated,

> I want to win ... Knowing we came close and were good [but] not good enough, that's what motivated all of us.[47]

Good Enough is Never Is. The goal is to get excuses out of our lives to win.

B. Making Excuses

"Our offensive line, our defensive line and now the
secondary, everyone — We're coming together as a team."[48]

— JAY CUTLER
CHICAGO BEARS QUARTERBACK

"Winning is only possible with massive actions."[49]

Making excuses are a part of our sinful human nature. From the earliest of our days, we find ways to avoid and/or get around what we are assigned to do. We are excuse makers, yet to win, we must take excessive actions.

An excuse (paraiteomai) is being reluctant about
a matter and begging for release.[50]

GENESIS 3:12
*"...the man said, **The woman** ... **she gave me** of the*
*tree, and **I did eat**."*

EXODUS 4:10
"And Moses said unto the LORD, ...
*'**I am not eloquent**, ... but **I am slow of speech**,*
and of a slow tongue.'"

JEREMIAH 1:6
"Then said I, Ah, Lord GOD! behold,
***I cannot speak**: for **I am a child**."*

> *"An excuse is a justification for doing*
> *— or not doing — something."*[51]

— GRANT CARDONE,

IN *THE 10X RULE,* PURPORTS THE FOLLOWING ABOUT EXCUSES:

Excuses are never the reason for why you did or didn't do something. They're just *a revision of the facts* that *you make up* in order to help yourself feel better about what happened (or didn't).[52]

The facts of our situations are what they are. An excuse is an unreasonable fact that I give to escape from a promised responsibility. An **excuse** is what I **"make up"** to get out of something I do not really want to do. Discipleship moves us **from excuses to the truth and facts** of our reality and gives us a reason to be responsible to what we are assigned to do.

THINK ABOUT IT!

In what way are we revising what the Lord has called

us to do _____.

Write the excuse you have for not doing what the

Lord directed you to do _____.

C. Excuse defined

1. An *excuse (paraiteomai)* is to *put something aside* for *something else*.[53]

2. An *excuse (egkataleipo)* is to *forsake, desert, abandon* and *leave behind*.[54]

State a reason you would forsake and abandon the Lord's work in your life _____.

Give one reason you would put aside following the Lord for something else _____.

An excuse (apologeomai) is to make a legal plea for oneself that has no defense.[55]

D. Man Made Excuses

1. Let Me First Bury My Father.

LUKE 9:59

"... Follow me. But he said, Lord, suffer me first to go and bury my father."

If you examine *every excuse* you have ever made, it centered in a *"me first"* mind set. To be *first (proton)* is to be of ***primary importance***.[56] The Lord is to be "first" and of primary importance in my life.

LUKE 9:59

*"... **Follow me**. But he said, Lord, **suffer me first to** go and **bury my father**."*

This young man's father was not dead, but aged? As possibly the eldest son of the family, he had a responsibility to stay at home and carry out the work his father could not do.

If his father had actually died, the reality is, the young man would not have been with the Lord Jesus. He would have been at home.

He asked to be excused from following the Lord until his aged father died, then he anticipated that he would be willing to follow.

Yet, there is no guarantee that he would follow later if he were unwilling to follow now.

THINK ABOUT IT!

Name a Man who delayed and followed the Lord

_____.

Name your excuse for not following the Lord _____

_____.

2. Let Me First Say Goodbye.

LUKE 9:61

"And another also said,
Lord, I will follow thee; but *let* **me first** *go bid them farewell, which are at home at my house."*

Here again is the *"me first"* idea that places the Lord in the second position. The word *first (rison)* means *to be the head.*[57] Often, we hear people saying, *"To the Lord who is the head of my life."* To be *first* is to be the *head*. If the Lord is *"first,"* and *"head,"* of your life, then *the Lord must give your life direction without question*.

Often we make excuses because the Lord is not "first" nor the "head" of my heart, my thinking, and my living.

LUKE 9:61

*"... **Lord, I will follow thee; but** let **me first** go bid them farewell, ... at home."*

This young man's excuse for not immediately following the Lord was that he wanted to say goodbye to his family. What do you think his family said to him? Do you think he came back?

THINK ABOUT IT!

Do you think his family would have made excuses

for him to stay at home? Explain _____

3. I Was Afraid.

> *To be afraid (deliao) is to be timid,*
> *to tremble, and to be scared.*[58]

Yes, you and I identify with the words "I was afraid,"
"timid," "tremble," and "scared." These are realities that
we experience daily. It is the *"afraid,"* in our lives, that
keeps us from moving from Good to Great.

> *"FEAR stands for False Events Appearing Real.*
> *[M]ost of what you are afraid of doesn't ever*
> *come to pass."*[59]

In **Matthew 25:14**, a Man was going on a journey
and he gave his employees a portion of money of his
business to invest for him until he returned. In **Matthew
25:25**, the third worker, buried the Man's money and
did not invest it. He did not even consider depositing it
into the bank to gain interest on the money.

When asked to **give an account** of his work, *the Man
gave the excuse, "**And I was afraid**."* It has been suggested

that *"Fear, for the most part, is provoked by emotions, not by rational thinking"*[60] and *faith* in God.

a. Frightened and Terrified

We *make excuses* because *we are frightened and terrified*. Excuses are for Men who *refuse to take responsibility* for their lives and how it turns out.[61]

THINK ABOUT IT!

Write an excuse you need to get out of your life

E. A No Excuse Man Has Peace

> *To be afraid (ekphobos) is to be terrified and frightened out of one's senses.*[62]

> *"Nothing happens to you; it happens because of you."*[63]

Consider the following thoughts before making another excuse.

1. No excuse can alter your situation or make your situation better.[64]

2. Refuse to make any more excuses and go out and search for the answers.[65]

3. Making excuses is a worthless use of your energy.[66]

PSALM 37:37

*"Mark **the perfect man**, ...
for **the end** of that man **is peace**."*

Who is a "perfect" man according to scripture?

1. A **perfect (tamiym)** man is **blameless**, upright, and righteous.[67]

2. A **perfect (selam)** man **fully finishes** the Lord's **temple work**.[68]

Psalm 37:37 declares that that **man's end (kalah)** is to **bring to completion** the awesome **goodness of God**.[69] The **upright** and **righteous man's end** is **peace**.

1. **Peace (salon)** is **tranquility** and **blessing** in your coming and going.[70]

2. **Peace (eirene)** is to having the **divine favor** of God **to prosper** in every kind of good.[71]

A No Excuse Man will **say "YES!"** to the **purposes of God** for his life. He will work to accomplish, finish, and bring to completion the purposes of God through his life.

Excuses are *"**not an option**,"* but completing *the purposes of God* is "your duty, obligation, and responsibility."[72]

Cardone further asserts,

> Do not use another excuse as the reason why the purpose of God did not come to fruition in your life, to your team, your family, your Church, or the world.[73]

Write an excuse that you have for not moving from

Good to Great _____.

CHAPTER 4

A Do Something Man

Can a Man
" ... stand in the street until change happens?"[74]
Don't just stand there, do something!

In the Monday, February 6, 2012, issue of the *Chicago Sun Times* was a reflective statement by a New England Patriots receiver who dropped a strategic catch in **Super Bowl 46**, that was played in Indianapolis, Indiana on Sunday, February 5, 2012.

Receiver **Wes Welker** couldn't believe he missed out on his chance when he dropped the ball.

"It's one of those plays I've made a thousand times. Just didn't make it. I've got to make the play. It comes to the biggest moment of my life, and I don't come up with it. It is discouraging. [A] most critical situation, and I let the team down."[75]

The reality of our existence is, when we try to "**Do Something**," sometimes we "**make the play**," and sometimes "**we don't make the play**." Each moment of our lives is a "**critical situation**." We must "*never give up*," but continue to "*live up*" to the challenge to "*help the team up*," even when we may occasionally "*let the team down*."

A. Making the Play

A **Do Something Man** gets into the game and does what he can. You will miss some plays, and drop some passes thrown to you. Those critical moments can be discouraging. Remember:

1. You will have other critical moments.

2. You will have other big opportunities.

3. You will be given tomorrow a time "to make the play."

4. "Keep coming to the game and trying [to win].[76]

A **Do Something Man** prepares through the instruction in the word of God, to know, and be prepared to move today and tomorrow into the purposes of God.

DEUTERONOMY 4:36

*"... he made thee to **hear his voice**, that **he might instruct** thee."*

PSALM 32:8

*"I will **instruct** thee and **teach** thee in **the way** which **thou shalt go**."*

B. Be Instructed to Do Something

Instruction (sakhal) gives insight on how to prosper.[77]

To **Do Something**, you must attend the Team Meetings. The meetings are the place of instruction, practice, and inspiration for the work that must be done. Many Men **drop the ball** because they **consistently miss the Practice** and the **Study of the Word** of God that gives us our position and the play and the route we are to run to Win the game.

Why we need to be instructed into Success.

1. Instruction teaches us what needs to be done.

2. It helps us to see the results that are expected.

3. It gives us insider change and transformation.[78]

THINK ABOUT IT!

Give one reason you need to be instructed in the word of God _____.

C. The Why of Instruction

Instruction pushes us to *"inspired standards"* that we can *"no longer stand mediocrity."* We can no longer accept that "good is good enough.[79]

Instruction *builds, creates, and contributes* God's potential for our lives. *Instruction* sparks us to further *inner development and maturation* that pushes us to *extraordinary* results.[80] Instruction moves us from *Good to Great* to grow and succeed in the purposes of God.

1. *Instruction (lamad)* is to be *trained* in *the ways of God*.[81]

2. *Instruction (yada)* leads us to *know* what to *do or think* in respect to God.[82]

3. *Instruction (paideuo) conforms* our will and action *to God's divine moral truth*.[83]

THINK ABOUT IT!

Tell how will you encourage a Man to be Instructed to Do Something _____.

To do (asah) something means to accomplish, complete, and perform[84] *the purposes of God.*

Every **Man of God** is called to **do something**. Often my **"Do Nothing"** is based on my **"unwillingness or refusal"** to be **taught and trained** in the work of the Lord Jesus Christ. Every Man must be taught God's Business is to Do Something.

D. The Bible's Do Something

To do (abad) something is to labor, to carry out and to be focused on changing something[85] *for the purposes of God.*

GENESIS 39:11

*"... And it came to pass ... that **Joseph** went into the house to **do his business**."*

EXODUS 20:9

*"**Six days** shalt thou **labour**, and **do all thy work**."*

EXODUS 24:3

*"... **All the words** which the LORD hath said **will we do**."*

NUMBERS 4:30

*"... every one that entereth into the service, ... **do the work** of the tabernacle."*

1 SAMUEL 26:25

*"Then Saul said to **David**, ... my son David: thou shalt
both **do great things**."*

PSALM 34:14

*"**Depart** from **evil**, and **do good**;
seek peace, and pursue it."*

PSALM 40:8

"I delight to do thy will, O my God."

John Kotter, in *A Sense of Urgency* calls every Man from complacency to action. He suggests the following:

1. **Set goals 10 yards at a time**. Name your 10 yard goal _____.

2. **Improve your serve**. Identify the service you can improve _____.

3. **Reposition yourself to be stretched more**. Write where you will stretch _____.

4. **Push beyond business as usual**. Name your God business _____.

5. **Experience the "Wow!" factor**.[86] Name the "Wow!" in your life _____.

"[Don't] hang a banner and ... pretend the mission [is] accomplished.

[Get] the job done."[87]

— RAHM ISRAEL EMANUEL,
MAYOR OF CHICAGO

Grant Cardone has suggested that we are often slow to "**do something**" because we have **not put much thought** or **effort** into what is **required to get the job done** successfully.[88]

To be a "**Do Something Man**," you must "*Keep taking action until you can't stop your forward momentum.*"[89] You must "Be ... wary of those who suggest you have done enough. Now is not the time for rest ... it's time for more action."[90]

The Lord Jesus declared in **Luke 2:49**, "... I must be about my Father's business."

To do (poieo) something is to produce and bring something to completion.[91]

A "**Do Something Man**" does not run in the face of fear, but he takes actions to succeed.

"[R]ather than seeing fear as a sign to run ... it must become your indicator to go."[92]

41

THINK ABOUT IT!

When can a Do Something Man say that he has done

enough _____.

Write what you need to do to succeed _____

_____.

E. Do the Necessary

"[Y]ou must stay committed to taking action ...
Even after achieving success along the way, continue to
take more actions in order to exceed your goals."[93]

A *"Do Something Man,"* as a rule, will *"assess the level of effort necessary* to realize a goal [and] ... *dare to dream* at levels previously unimaginable."[94]

THINK ABOUT IT!

Write one necessary effort you must do to reach a

Man outside the Men's fellowship _____.

> *To move from Good to Great,*
> *"always put forth 10 times the amount of activity that*
> *others do."*[95]

F. Men Who Did Something

The Bible is a call to *"**Do Something**."* We must be *"trained properly"* in the Lord's Word. In the Bible, and in our lives, "Nothing happens without action. ... The time is always now to take action."[96]

> *"[B]y the time you get yourself 'ready' to do something,*
> *someone else has taken action – and now you are*
> *regretting it."*[97]

Examine Biblical Men who took action and did something.

GENESIS 12:5

*"And **Abram** took Sarai his wife, and Lot ... and **they went forth** to go into the land of Canaan."*

Name the Lord's "went forth to go into" that you are

to do _____.

EXODUS 4:21

*"... **Moses** ... **do all those wonders** before Pharaoh, which I have put in thine hand."*

A wonder (pele) is a deed of God to deliver and move people to worship.[98]

The Lord has put wonders in our hands to deliver people. Do something.

JUDGES 6:14

*"And **the LORD looked upon** [Gideon], and said, **Go** ... **save Israel** ..."*

Name the place where you are to go save _____

_____.

1 SAMUEL 17:32

*"And **David** said **to Saul**, ... **thy servant will go and fight** with this Philistine [Goliath]."*

Name the fight you are to do today and tomorrow

_____.

MARK 5:19

*"... **Go home** ... and **tell them** how **great things** the Lord hath done for thee."*

"It's far preferable to fail while doing something than to fail"[96] by doing nothing.

THINK ABOUT IT!

Name something you did not complete. Get up and

do something _____.

CHAPTER 5

A Successful Man

*"Look around, and ... you'll see
a world filled with average."*[100]

Often our lives begin in average. Average is "half way." We are socialized to accept average as good enough. "Average ... assumes less than extraordinary."[101] *Average* may be where you start, but *average* is not where you stop.

You were not created by God to exist in average. In *The 10X Rule*, Cardone asserts that *average* is defined as an *"acceptable level of activity."*[102] *Average* is *"taking normal action"* and being *"fine with it".*[103] Your *"addiction to average"* can keep you from your possibility.[104]

> *"Success is your duty.*
> *[It] provides confidence ... in terms of what is possible."*[105]

THINK ABOUT IT!

Name one action you can take right now to get out

of average _____.

A. Biblical Success

> *You will never have success*
> *if you are content and complacent.*
> *Your inevitable end will be decline.*[106]

To **succeed** there must be a **continuous push** toward progress. To stimulate change and improvement, it must come from within us. We must constantly bring discomfort into our lives to combat our complacency.[107]

It is the Word of God that pushes us forward. The Word of God "stimulates change" in our lives. The Word of God "combats our complacency" and leads us to be "prosperous" and to have "good success."

Read what the Lord said to Joshua about "good success."

JOSHUA 1:8

*"This book of **the law**; ...**meditate therein day and night**, ... **observe to do** ... for then thou shalt **make thy way prosperous**, and then **thou shalt have good success**."*

What is good success?

"[S]uccess [is] something that's created
—not acquired.
[S]uccess is something people make."[108]

Success (qum) is standing up, rising up, recovering, enduring, and being victorious[109] in the purposes of God.

THINK ABOUT IT!

Name what the Lord is calling you to stand up for

_____.

Identify what or who you are to recover _____

_____.

B. Getting Out of Average

*"We should have won that football game ...
We gave up too many big plays... .
That's why we didn't win."*[110]

BRIAN URLACHER,
MIDDLE LINEBACKER, CHICAGO BEARS

In the book, *Unleash the Warrior Within,* it was quoted, "... if one advances confidently in the direction of his dreams ... he will meet with a success unexpected in common hours."[111] To **get out of average**, you must **advance forward** with confidence; you must **do what everyone else refuses to do**; you must "[**embrace**] a **greater-than-average thought** and action process."[112]

*You must stop "... waiting for success and ...
approach it as [an] ... obligation and responsibility."*[113]

"Accepting average won't get the job done."[114]

C. Moving Toward Success

"One play can change the complexity of the game."[115]
Ray, Chaplain for the Chicago Bears

To **move toward success**, Richard Machowicz says you must **"Do something"** to get a result. He asserts:

1. ***Focus*** your mind on your target.

2. Without focus your results will be happenstance and unreliable.

3. "Get everything out of the way of the target."

4. ***Decide*** on your ***goals*** and the ***tools and people*** you need to ***achieve it***.[116]

THINK ABOUT IT!

Write your "do something" to move you toward

success _____.

D. State Your Goal

It is hard work not succeeding. Change your focus.
Go after success as your calling and duty.
Never retreat, be constant, persistent,
and attack the target.[117]

What are the benefits of stating your goal? A goal is a mechanism for you to grow and prosper.

1. A goal offers you a way to innovate.

2. A goal helps to produce something that has never been done.

3. A goal is an opportunity for you to improve and move from where you are.

4. A goal pushes you to improve, to not relax, and to do better.[118]

THINK ABOUT IT!

Write your personal goal and Mission for the Lord

_____

Read the following Biblical Goals

EXODUS 14:15

*"... Moses, ... **speak** unto the children of Israel, that they **go forward**."*

State where you must go forward _____

_____

NUMBERS 13:30

*"And **Caleb** ... **said, Let us go up at once**, and possess it; for we are well able to overcome it."*

Write what you must do at once to overcome it _____

_____.

MARK 1:38

"And he said unto them, **Let us go into the next towns***, that I may preach there also: for therefore came I forth."*

Identify where you must go and do to fulfill God's

purpose _____.

Consider the following:

1. When you reach one goal it compels you to set a loftier goal.[119]
2. Success is the result of earlier actions and countless actions taken over a period of time.[120]

To succeed, you cannot just do one thing, you must do many things, in many ways, as with many people that you can to reach your goal.

— ROGERS W. JACKSON

THINK ABOUT IT!

Write the actions you are taking to succeed _____

_____.

Success (sakhal) is to act with insight, to prosper, to know,
understand, and comprehend what the end will be.[121]

E. Push beyond Average

"Create more success than you need ... you are never safe to
move to normal levels of involvement and activity.
Normal gets you just that — normal."[122]

To **Get Out of Average**, do the following.

1. Use your personal energy, resources, and
    creativity to take massive action to get the job
    done.

2. Take in consideration the efforts of others to
    impede your efforts.

3. Realize that others will take from you what
    they cannot create for themselves.

4. Be aware that you will face conditions that are
    hostile to your progress.

5. Plan to succeed so big that no person, event, or
    series of missteps can stop you.[123]

To **Get Out of Average**, realize that others are not
on your schedule. Everyone has their agenda and plan.
Everyone has a project they are trying to complete.
To succeed, you must put forth "enormous effort and

persistence ... considerations and ways of thinking [and] ... massive amounts of acts that are necessary to push through."[124]

Take the following actions:

1. Push to increased actions. Do more.
2. Do not prepare for normal conditions, but prepare for resistance.
3. Rid yourself of average advice.
4. Get around Men who see it is their duty, obligation, and responsibility to be exceptional thinkers and doers.[125]

Average is not an option.
"Average anything will never get you to
an extraordinary life."[126]

Endnotes

1   Jim Collins and Morten Hansen, *Great by Choice* (New York, NY: Harper Collins Publishers, 2011), 1.

2   Neil Hayes, "Leader Rose Starts Strong," *Chicago Sun Times*, 27 December 2011, 57.

3   Ibid.

4   Ibid.

5   John Oxenham, "The Ways," Retrieved from Internet, Thursday, December 8, 2011 (http://www.ldssplash.com/gospeltopics/free_agency/ways.htm)

6   Warren Baker and Eugene Carpenter, *The Complete Word Study Dictionary: Old Testament* (Chattanooga, TN: AMG Publishers, 2003), 185.

7   Sean Jensen, "Bears General Manager A Man of Many Hats," *Chicago Sun Times*, 31 January 2012, 52.

8   Ibid., 1204.

9   Spiros Zodhiates, *The Complete Word Study Dictionary: New Testament* (Chattanooga, TN: AMG Publishers, 1992), 429.

10   Sean Jensen, 52.

11   Mark Potash, "Emory Shows Love to Lovie," *Chicago*

     Sun Times, 31 January 2012, 53.

12   Jensen, 52.

13   Lauren Fitzpatrick, "Busted Bear Released from Jail – And from Team," *Chicago Sun Times*, 17 December 2011, 6.

14   Ibid.

15   Natasha Korecki, Lauren Fitzpatrick, and Abdon Pallasch, "My Life is in Ruins," *Chicago Sun Times*, 8 December 2011, 2.

16   Ibid.

17   Ibid.

18   Neil Hayes, "Take Boozer for What He Is," *Chicago Sun Times*, 27 January 2012, 60.

19   Collins and Hansen, *Great by Choice*, 2.

20   Ibid., 2, 3.

21   Baker and Carpenter, 127.

22   Zodhiates, 98.

23   Ibid., 187.

24   Baker and Carpenter, 974.

25   Jim Collins, *Good to Great* (New York, NY: Harper Collins Publishers, 2001), 21.

26   Zodhiates, 98.

27   Ibid., 367.

28   Baker and Carpenter, 1217.

29   Zodhiates, 936.

30   Herbert Lockyer, *All the Men of the Bible* (Grand Rapids, MI: Zondervan Publishing Company, 1952), 50.

31   Collins, *Good to Great*, 20.

32   Baker and Carpenter, 541.

33   Ibid., 254.

34   Zodhiates, 1448.

35   Ibid., 221.

36   Ibid., 221.

37   Ibid., 475.

38   Ibid.

39   Ibid., 476.

40   Sean Jenson, "The Legacy Remains Intact," *Chicago Sun Times*, 6 February 2012, 60.

41   Jim Collins and Jerry Porras, *Built to Last* (New York, NY: Harper Collins Publishers, 2004), 185.

42   Ibid., 186.

43   Ibid., 187.

44   Ibid.

45   Ibid., 188.

46   Ibid.

47   Neil Hayes, "Boozer Driven by Criticism," *Chicago Sun Times*, 8 December 2011, 67.

48   Neil Hayes, "This Group Full of Stars, Full of Hits," *Chicago Sun Times*, 15 November 2011, 60.

49   Grant Cardone, *The 10X Rule: The Only Difference Between Success and Failure* (Hoboken, NJ: John Wiley and Sons, Inc., 2011), 109.

50   Zodhiates, 1105.

51   Cardone, 155.

52   Ibid., 55, 156.

53   Zodhiates, 1105.

54   Ibid., 499.

55   Ibid., 232.

56 Ibid., 1247.

57 Baker and Carpenter, 1027.

58 Zodhaites, 401.

59 Cardone, 116.

60 Ibid.

61 Ibid., 156.

62 Zodhiates, 558.

63 Ibid., 157.

64 Ibid.

65 Ibid., 157.

66 Ibid., 158.

67 Baker and Carpenter, 1232.

68 Ibid., 1152

69 Ibid., 507.

70 Ibid., 1145.

71 Zodhiates, 519.

72 Cardone, 158.

73 Ibid.

74 Neil Steinberg, "Occupy Chicago Joins the Party," *Chicago Sun Times*, 18 November 2011, 16.

75 Sean Jensen, "The Legacy Remains Intact," *Chicago Sun Times*, 6 February 2012, 60.

76 Ibid.

77 Baker and Carpenter, 1137.

78 Collins, *Good to Great*, 30, 32.

79 Ibid., 31.

80 Ibid., 36, 37.

81 Baker and Carpenter, 551.

82   Ibid., 420.

83   Zodhiates, 1088.

84   Baker and Carpenter, 876.

85   Ibid., 795.

86   John Kotter, *A Sense of Urgency* (Boston, MA: Harvard Business Press, 2008), 134.

87   Abond M. Pallashch, Rahm Lights into Mitt in Iowa," *Chicago Sun Times*, 20 November 2011, 3A.

88   Cardone, 1.

89   Ibid., 110.

90   Ibid.

91   Zodhaites, 1187.

92   Ibid., 116.

93   Cardone, 110.

94   Ibid., 1.

95   Ibid., 2.

96   Ibid., 117.

97   Ibid.

98   Baker and Carpenter, 899.

99   Ibid.

100 Cardone, 61.

101 Ibid., 52.

102 Ibid.

103 Ibid., 53, 52.

104 Ibid.

105 Ibid., 22.

106 Collins and Porras, *Built to Last*, 187.

107 Ibid., 187, 188.

108 Cardone, 34.

109 Baker and Carpenter, 987.

110 Sean Jensen, "Blunts Fast Finish," *Chicago Sun Times*, 28 November 2011, 3.

111 Richard Machowicz, *Unleash the Warrior Within* (Philadelphia, PA: Da Capo Press, 2008), 21.

112 Cardone, 62.

113 Ibid., 25.

114 Ibid., 63.

115 The Chicago Bears Chaplain, "Ray" was interviewed on a religious radio broadcast following the Chicago Bears Sunday night loss on Kansas City Chiefs, Sunday, December 4, 2011.

116 Machowicz, 22, 23.

117 Cardone, 55.

118 Collins and Porras, *Built to Last*, 188.

119 Cardone, 28.

120 Ibid., 29.

121 Baker and Carpenter, 1137

122 Cardone, 64.

123 Ibid., 63, 64.

124 Ibid., 65.

125 Ibid., 66, 67.

126 Ibid., 67.

Bibliography

Baker, Warren and Carpenter, Eugene. *The Complete Word Study Dictionary: Old Testament*. Chattanooga, TN: AMG Publishers, 2003.

Collins, Jim. *Good to Great.* New York, NY: Harper Collins Publishers, 2001.

Collins, Jim and Hansen, Morten. *Great by Choice.* New York, NY: Harper Collins Publishers, 2011.

Collins, Jim and Porras, Jerry. *Built to Last: Successful Habits of Visionary Companies.* New York, NY: Harper Collins Publishers, 2004.

Grant Cardone, *The 10X Rule: The Only Difference Between Success and Failure*. Hoboken, NJ: John Wiley and Sons, Inc., 2011.

Kotter, John. *A Sense of Urgency.* Boston, MA: Harvard Business Press, 2008.

Lockyer, Herbert. *All the Men of the Bible.* Grand Rapids, MI:
    Zondervan Publishing Company, 1952.

Machowicz, Richard. *Unleash the Warrior Within.*
    Philadelphia, PA: Da Capo Press, 2008.

Oxenham, John. "The Ways," Retrieved from Internet,
    Thursday, December 8, 2011 (http://www.ldssplash.
    com/gospeltopics/free_agency/ways.htm).

Zodhiates, Spiros. *The Complete Word Study Dictionary: New
    Testament.* Chattanooga, TN: AMG Publishers, 1992.